CONTENTS

5 Introduction
6 Word list

7 What are materials?

8 What are materials? questions...... *(higher level)*
9 What are materials? questions...... *(lower level)*
10 Sorting stuff...... *(chart filling)*
11 Material clues...... *(vocabulary game)*
12 Match it...... *(matching pictures with words)*

13 Natural or manufactured?...... *(recount)*

14 Natural or manufactured? questions...... *(higher level)*
15 Natural or manufactured? questions...... *(lower level)*
16 My materials pictures...... *(sorting)*
17 My materials chart...... *(sorting)*
18 Connections...... *(vocabulary)*

19 Sorting and grouping...... *(report)*

20 Sorting and grouping questions...... *(higher level)*
21 Sorting and grouping questions...... *(lower level)*
22 Starters and endings...... *(matching sentence starters to endings)*
23 Describing materials...... *(drawing, naming, describing)*
24 Firm or runny?...... *(sorting and grouping)*
25 Magnetic or not?...... *(investigating and reporting)*
26 What goes where?...... *(labelling materials)*

27 What's it made of?...... *(recount)*

28 What's it made of? questions...... *(higher level)*
29 What's it made of? questions...... *(lower level)*
30 The right material...... *(matching, labelling)*
31 Eating materials...... *(extracting information from lists)*
32 What is it? ...... *(matching words to clues)*

CONTENTS

33 What's it like?...... *(recount)*
34 What's it like? questions...... *(higher level)*
35 What's it like? questions...... *(lower level)*
36 Properties crossword...... *(word building)*
37 What must it be?...... *(word selection)*
38 Useful things...... *(matching pictures to labels; grouping)*
39 Putting things right...... *(classifying on a Carroll diagram)*
40 Tell me about it...... *(describing)*

41 What shall we use?...... *(factual)*
42 What shall we use? questions...... *(higher level)*
43 What shall we use? questions...... *(lower level)*
44 Materials wordsearch...... *(understanding vocabulary)*

45 Changing shape...... *(table, diagrams)*
46 Changing shape questions...... *(higher level)*
47 Changing shape questions...... *(lower level)*
48 Bending, twisting, stretching and squashing...... *(interpreting text)*

49 Hot and cold...... *(factual)*
50 Hot and cold questions...... *(higher level)*
51 Hot and cold questions...... *(lower level)*
52 Melt down...... *(interpreting graphical information)*
53 Melt down graph...... *(interpreting graphical information)*
54 All change...... *(describing, giving examples)*

55 Test it...... *(instructions)*
56 Test it questions...... *(higher level)*
57 Test it questions...... *(lower level)*
58 Getting wet...... *(reporting on an investigation)*
59 Our wetting materials chart...... *(reporting on an investigation)*
60 Handling things...... *(using vocabulary)*

61 Water...... *(posters)*
62 Water questions...... *(higher level)*
63 Water questions...... *(lower level)*
64 Using water...... *(interpreting pictures)*

INTRODUCTION

Children often struggle to remember science words. Sometimes the words seem strange or unusual, and sometimes the words we use in science have other meanings in everyday life. Think about these science words: *material, property, hard, soft*. If you ask a child what these words mean, you are likely to get responses such as: 'My coat is made of material'; 'My things are my property'; 'These sums are too hard for me'; 'You won't do that because you're soft'. But when children go into science lessons, we sometimes assume that they already understand a 'material' to be any substance, a 'property' to be how a material behaves, and 'hard' or 'soft' to be words that describe specific properties of a material.

Scientific language

This series aims to give children practice in using science words, both through science activities and in 'real life' contexts, so that they become familiar with the scientific meanings of these words. Use of the correct scientific vocabulary is essential for high attainment in SATs. The QCA *Scheme of Work for Science* (DfES) for Key Stages 1 and 2 in England suggests examples of vocabulary for each of its units; although these books are not divided into exactly the same topics, the QCA vocabulary and its progressive introduction are used as the basis for the word selection here.

The science covered is divided into units based on topics from the national curricula for England, Wales, Scotland and Northern Ireland. In this book, the science is drawn from the 'Materials and their properties' statements for ages 6–7 relating to grouping materials and changing materials. The series of boxed letters at the bottom of each page shows in which curriculum documents the focus of each activity occurs. For example, for the activity on page 61, the boxes E NI W S indicate that the activity focuses on a topic from the Scottish Guidelines only.

Science and literacy

The National Literacy Strategy for England suggests teaching objectives and gives examples of the types of activities that children should encounter during each year of primary school. This book uses many of these techniques for developing children's understanding and use of scientific language. The activities here are mainly intended for use in science time, as they have been written with science learning objectives in mind. However, some of the activities could be used in literacy time. Science texts have already been published for use in literacy time, but many of them use science content appropriate for older children. During literacy time you need to be focusing on language skills, not teaching new science. It is with this in mind that these sheets, drawing from age-appropriate science work, have been produced. It is also suggested that these sheets are used in literacy time only after the science content has been introduced in science time.

The series focuses mainly on paper-based activities to develop scientific language, rather than experimental and investigative work, but it is hoped that teachers might use some of the ideas in planning practical science activities.

About this book

Each unit in this book begins with a non-fiction text that introduces some key scientific vocabulary. The key words are highlighted by bold type. The texts cover a range of non-fiction genres.

Following this text are two comprehension activities that help children to identify and understand the key words (and introduce some new science words). They are pitched at two levels:

 for older or more able children

 for younger or less able children.

Although the comprehension activities are designed to be used mainly during science time, you may wish to use the texts as examples of non-fiction texts in literacy time. The comprehension pages contain two or three types of question (a change of icon indicates a change in the type of question):

 The answer can be found in the text.

 Children will need to think about the answer. These questions usually elicit science understanding beyond what the text provides.

 An activity aimed at developing the children's literacy skills. These are optional extension activities for individual or group work, with teacher support if necessary.

Following the comprehension pages in each unit are activities aimed at developing children's understanding and use of the key vocabulary and additional science vocabulary. Strategies used include: making and completing diagrams, charts and tables; description; matching pictures and writing; labelling; sequencing; analysing graphs and tables; matching sentence starters to endings; identifying true and false statements; word grids and wordsearches; matching words and meanings; making connections; picture interpretation; and some easily set up practical activities.

WORD LIST

alive	freeze	not magnetic	stone
aluminium	glass	object	stretch
bend	hard	paper	stretched
bending	harder	plastic	stretching
bent	harmful	pollute	strong
boil	heated	pour	substance
cardboard	heavy	properties	taste
clean	hot	rock	thin
cling film	ice	rough	tough
coal	iron	rust	transparent
cold	leather	scratched	twist
conserve	light	shape	twisted
cooler	liquid	shiny	twisting
cotton	litter	smell	warmer
dry	look	smooth	water
dull	magnet	soft	waterproof
feather	magnetic	solid	wet
feature	manufactured	sort	wood
feel	material	squash	wooden
fertiliser	medicine	squashed	wool
flat	melt	squashing	woollen
flexible	metal	steam	
foam	natural	steel	
foil	never alive	stiff	

What are materials?

Materials are the things that something can be made from.
Most materials are either **solid** or **liquid**.
Some materials were once **alive**.
Some materials were **never alive**.
Living things are made of materials that are alive now.

Wood and **cotton** are dead materials, but they were once alive as parts of a plant.

wood

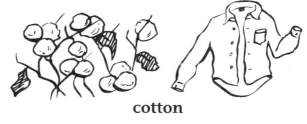
cotton

Wool and **feathers** are dead materials.
Once they were alive as parts of an animal.

wool

feathers

Rocks and **water** are materials that have never been alive.

Rocks are **solid**. Water is a **liquid**.
Wood, cotton, wool, feathers, rocks and water are all **natural** materials.
Some materials are made by people.
These materials are **manufactured**.
Glass, **paper** and **plastic** are all manufactured materials.

glass
plastic
paper

Photocopiable

What are materials?

1. What are **materials**? _____
   _____

2. Fill in the missing words in these sentences:

   Most materials are either _____ or _____.

   _____ and _____ are materials that have never been alive.

3. Circle the materials that were once alive.

   cotton   water   wool   wood   rock   feathers

4. Make up a sentence of your own, using all of these words:

   glass   paper   materials   plastic   manufactured

   _____
   _____

5. Water is a **liquid**. Name two other liquids.
   _____

6. List eight different materials found in your classroom.
   _____
   _____

7. Choose one **natural** material and one **manufactured** material. Draw a large picture of each material on the back of this sheet.

Find out what these words mean. Use a dictionary to help you.

   alive   solid   liquid   natural   manufactured

SCHOLASTIC
DEVELOPING SCIENCE LANGUAGE for Materials and their properties with 6–7 year olds

What are materials?

1. Complete this sentence:

   Materials are the things that _____

   _____

2. True or false? Tick the correct box.

   All materials are **solid**.   T ☐   F ☐

   Some materials were once **alive**.   T ☐   F ☐

   Living things are made of materials that are alive now.   T ☐   F ☐

3. Name one material that is **natural**. _____

4. Name one material that is **manufactured**. _____

5. Write the missing letters in these sentences:

   Wo __ d and cot __ on were once part of a pl __ nt.

   W __ ol and fe __ th __ rs were once part of an ani __ al.

6. Find and draw two things in your classroom that have been made from a **natural** material. Name each one.

Find out what these words mean. Use a dictionary to help you.

alive   solid   liquid

Sorting stuff

Some **materials** are made from things that were once **alive**. Some **materials** are made from things that have **never been alive**.

Look at these pictures of materials. Write their names in the correct columns on the chart at the bottom of the page.

once alive	never alive

Material clues

Work with a friend to solve these clues. You will both need a pencil and a copy of this sheet.

Set A clues

1. Plants grow well in this.
2. Makes your car go.
3. Like paper but stiffer.
4. Candles are made of this.
5. Keeps a dog warm.
6. Another word for 'cloth'.

Set B clues

1. Helps you to keep clean.
2. A valuable metal.
3. Used for colouring pictures.
4. A bird grows this.
5. Solid, black and burns well.
6. A common metal.

Word list

feather   fabric   card   powder paint
petrol   wax   gold   coal
soap   iron   soil   hair

Answers	
1.	4.
2.	5.
3.	6.

COVER THESE INSTRUCTIONS WHEN PHOTOCOPYING.

Teacher instructions
Agree who in each pair will read out the Set A clues and who will read out the Set B clues. The child who reads out the Set A clues must try to find the correct answers (from the word list) to the Set B clues, and vice versa. Each child must write the answers carefully in the correct spaces in the answer box on his or her sheet. To make sure that the children understand, it might be useful to work through one example from each set of clues with two volunteers and enlarged copies of this sheet.

Match it

What are these objects made of?
Draw a line to join each object to the right material.

Be careful! Look at all the objects before you draw any lines.

cotton

aluminium

rubber

glass

plastic

iron

leather

paper

Natural or manufactured?

Class 2 is taught by Mrs Twigg. Mrs Twigg is very good at teaching science. All the children in the class like her science lessons very much. They always learn something new.

One morning, Mrs Twigg taught the children about the difference between **natural** and **manufactured** materials. She made the lesson simple. She asked the children to remember just two things:

1. **Natural** materials are made by nature.
2. **Manufactured** materials are made by people.

She held up a chart for the children to look at. On the chart were the names of ten materials. Mrs Twigg's chart is shown on the right. Together, Mrs Twigg and the children read the names of the materials.

Materials chart	
natural	manufactured
coal	paper
wool	plastic
rock	cardboard
leather	steel
water	glass

Then Mrs Twigg held up a feather and a wooden ruler. She wanted to know where to write their names on the chart. Can you do it for her?

Natural or manufactured?

1. Which subject is Mrs Twigg very good at teaching? Write your answer as a full sentence.

   _____

2. Circle the correct word.

   A **natural** material is made by **people / nature**.

3. Connect each word to the correct box.

   coal | natural | paper
   cardboard | | stone
   leather | manufactured | glass

4. Under each material, write whether it is **natural** or **manufactured**.

   bone   brick   clay
   _____   _____   _____

   concrete   feather   Plasticine
   _____   _____   _____

5. Write another name for a table or diagram that gives information. It is a _____.

6. Sort out each set of mixed-up letters to make a word found on Mrs Twigg's chart. Write the word after each set of letters.

   twera   rehlate   spatcil

Make a collage picture, using only **natural** materials. Make a list of the materials you used and say why you used them where you did.

Natural or manufactured?

1. Which subject is Mrs Twigg very good at teaching? _____

2. How many things does Mrs Twigg ask the children to remember? _____

3. Finish each of these sentences.
   - **Natural** materials are _____
   - **Manufactured** materials are _____
   - On Mrs Twigg's chart were _____
   _____

4. Tick the **natural** materials in this list.
   - wool ◯
   - metal ◯
   - plastic ◯
   - glass ◯
   - rock ◯
   - coal ◯

5. Draw and write the name of one **natural** material and one **manufactured** material that are not on Mrs Twigg's chart.

natural	manufactured

Make a collage picture, using only **natural** materials. As well as these materials, you will need **stiff card** and **glue**. Make a list of the materials used and display it with your work.

Photocopiable

My materials pictures

What you need: the materials chart on page 17, crayons, scissors, paste.

What to do
1. Cut out each picture carefully.
2. Paste each picture into the correct column on your materials chart.
3. Write the name of each material in the box under its picture.

stone

glass

plastic

feather

cork

cardboard

bone

Plasticine

Enlarge to A3 size if required.

DEVELOPING SCIENCE LANGUAGE for Materials and their properties with 6–7 year olds

Photocopiable

My materials chart

2

Name _____ Class _____

| natural | manufactured |

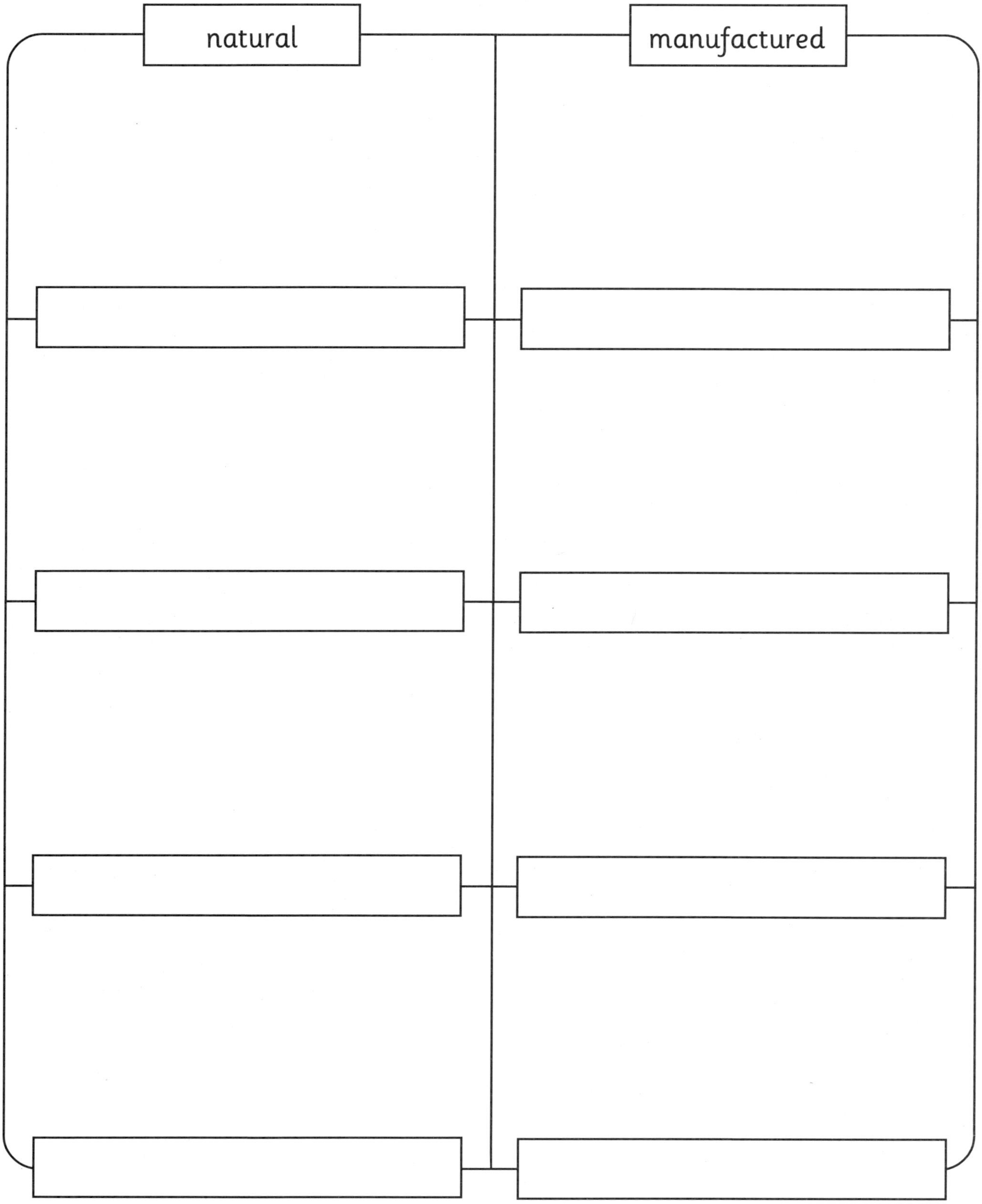

Enlarge to A3 size if required.

SCHOLASTIC
DEVELOPING SCIENCE LANGUAGE for Materials and their properties with 6–7 year olds

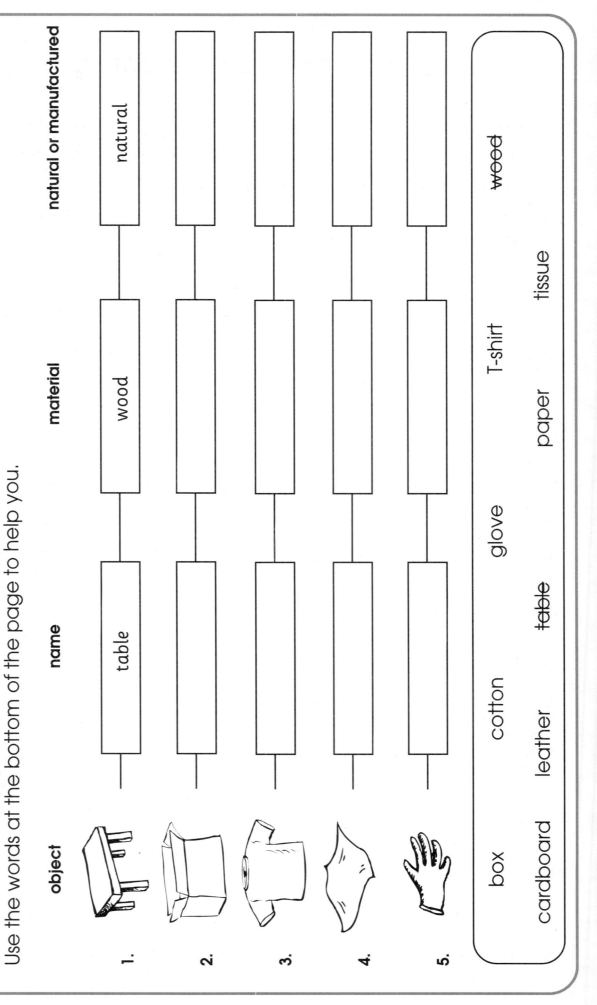

Sorting and grouping

Two groups of children were learning about **materials**. Each group had to **sort** these **objects** into two sets: an **aluminium** kettle, a **solid foam** sponge, a piece of **plastic** bubble wrap, an **iron** nail, a **woollen** jumper, a **wooden** ruler and a **steel** teaspoon.

This is what Nasreen's group wrote:

We have put the kettle, nail and teaspoon into one set because they are **metals**. We have put the sponge, bubble wrap, jumper and ruler into another set because they are **not metals**.

This is what Amjad's group wrote:

The kettle, nail, ruler and teaspoon are all **hard**, but the sponge, bubble wrap and jumper are all **soft**.

Mrs Twigg, their teacher, told Nasreen and Amjad that both the groupings were correct. The children had found out that materials can be grouped in different ways.

Sorting and grouping

1. How many groups of children were learning about **materials**? _____

2. List three of the **objects** the children were **sorting**.
   _____
   _____
   _____

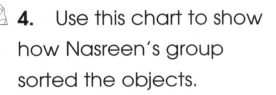

3. Which **material** was each of these objects made from?

bubble wrap	teaspoon	jumper
_____	_____	_____
sponge	nail	kettle
_____	_____	_____

4. Use this chart to show how Nasreen's group sorted the objects.

5. Think of some other objects that could be added to Nasreen's chart. Write them in the correct columns.

metal	non-metal

Think of a different way to **sort** the objects. Write your two sets on the back of this sheet. Explain how you have sorted them.

Sorting and grouping

1. How many groups of children were learning about **materials**? _____

2. Connect each **object** to the material that it is made from. One has been done for you.

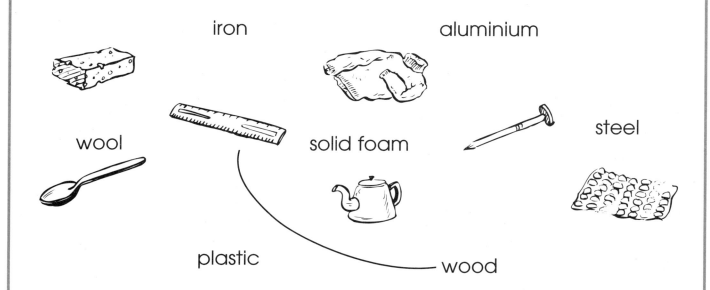

3. Name two other objects made from **metal**.

_____   _____

4. Fill in this chart to show Amjad's results.

hard				
soft				

Now sort the same objects into these two sets: **smooth** and **rough**. Draw two boxes on the back of this sheet to write the objects in.

Starters and endings

Match each sentence starter to the correct ending.

Objects that **float**	is not very bright to look at.
Rough materials	have an even surface.
A **shiny** surface	can be tested with your nose.
Objects that **sink**	have an uneven surface.
A **dull** surface	lets you see through it.
Smooth materials	drop to the bottom of water.
The **smell** of something	looks bright and glossy.
A **transparent** material	rest on the top of water.

Make up your own endings to these sentences.

A **hard** object is _____

A **soft** object is _____

Describing materials

Find **three** small objects in the classroom that are made from different materials. Use the chart below to draw and describe each object. You can use the words at the bottom of the page to describe your objects, or choose your own words.

1. Draw your object here.	2.	3.
Write its name here.		
What material is it made of?		
Write some words to describe your object here.		

| dull | shiny | hard | soft | rough | smooth | strong | weak | bendy |

Firm or runny?

Crisps and **biscuits** are **firm**. Something that is firm is called a **solid**.
Water and **milk** are **runny**. Something that is runny is called a **liquid**.

Sort these foods into **solids** and **liquids**. Write the name of each food, or draw a picture of it, in the correct column on the chart.

solids	liquids

How can you tell that orange juice, milk, lemonade and cola are **liquids**?

_____

Why are bread, carrots, cake and apples called **solids**?

_____

Name four other **solid** foods.

_____

Name four other **liquids** of any kind.

_____

Magnetic or not?

You will need a **magnet** and the eight things shown in the pictures.

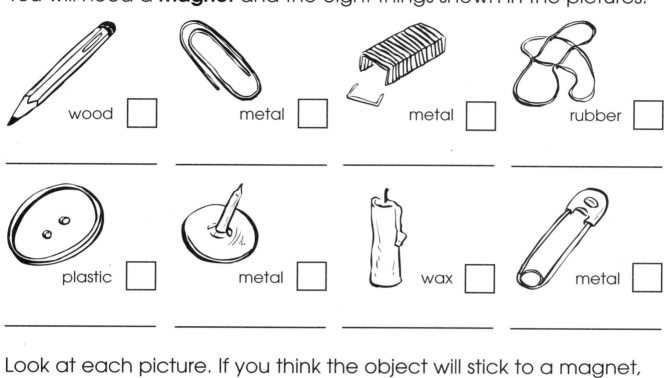

| wood ☐ | metal ☐ | metal ☐ | rubber ☐ |
| plastic ☐ | metal ☐ | wax ☐ | metal ☐ |

Look at each picture. If you think the object will stick to a magnet, put a tick by the picture. This is called making a **prediction**.

Test each object with the magnet.
Write **magnetic** under the pictures of things that stick to the magnet.
Write **not magnetic** under the pictures of things that do not stick to the magnet.

Were all your predictions correct? _____

What do you notice about the things that stick to the magnet?
_____

You should have found that **wood, rubber, plastic** and **wax** are not magnetic materials. Can you think of any others?
_____

What goes where?

Look at this list of materials. Now write the name of each material in the correct place on the picture. One has been written for you.

| paper | glass | plastic | cardboard | sand |
| leather | rubber | stone | cotton | steel |

Choose another material that could be used to do each job. You can choose from the list at the top of the page, or from any other materials you know.

1. _____
2. _____
3. _____
4. _____
5. _____

6. _____
7. _____
8. ___rubber (boots)_____
9. _____
10. _____

Enlarge this page to A3 size and use it for a group activity.

DEVELOPING SCIENCE LANGUAGE for Materials and their properties with 6–7 year olds

What's it made of?

Kelly and Darren made a model house.
They got the idea from a television programme.

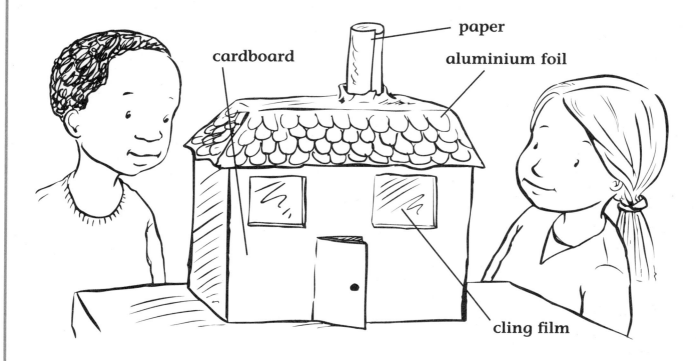

They used many different **materials** to build their house. For the walls, they used **stiff cardboard**. The cardboard was **light** in weight and **strong**.

The chimney was made from a tube of **paper**. The paper was **flexible** and easy to **bend** into **shape**.

Aluminium foil was used for the roof. The foil was **flat** and **smooth**. They **scratched** it to make a pattern of squares that looked like roof tiles. They painted the roof red to make it **look** like a real roof.

With their Mum's help, they cut holes in the cardboard walls. The holes looked like windows. They covered the windows with **cling film**. The cling film was **thin** and **transparent**, so it looked like **glass**.

They cut a flap in the cardboard in one wall to make a door that they could open and close.

Photocopiable

What's it made of?

1. Name the **materials** Kelly and Darren used to build the house.
   _____

2. Which one of the **materials** was:

   • **flat, smooth** and easily **scratched**? _____

   • **thin** and **transparent**? _____

   • **light** in weight and **strong**? _____

3. Choose a **material** from the list below that Darren and Kelly could also have used to make the:

   walls   chimney   roof   windows
   _____   _____   _____   _____

   | wood   fur   clay   chalk   fabric   water |
   | wax   card   wool   cotton   cellophane |

4. Name a **material** that each of these things could be made from.

_____   _____   _____

On another sheet of paper write instructions for making a model sailing boat. List the materials you would need.
Draw the boat. Label your drawing.

What's it made of?

1. Fill in the missing words.

   - The **cardboard** used by the children was _____ in weight and _____ .
   - **Paper** is _____ enough to _____ into **shape** easily.
   - **Aluminium foil** is _____ and _____ .
   - **Cling film** is _____ and _____ .

2. Tick the **material** used to make the:

walls	stiff cardboard	☐	cling film	☐
chimney	aluminium foil	☐	paper tube	☐
roof	paper tube	☐	aluminium foil	☐
windows	cling film	☐	stiff cardboard	☐

3. Write what **material** might be used to make:

   - a bicycle frame _____
   - a table _____

   If you don't know, ask an adult or look in a book.

Write instructions for making a model sailing boat. List the materials you would need. Draw the boat. Label your drawing.

The right material

Draw a line connecting each picture to the name of the material it is made from. Then write the name below the picture. The first one has been done for you.

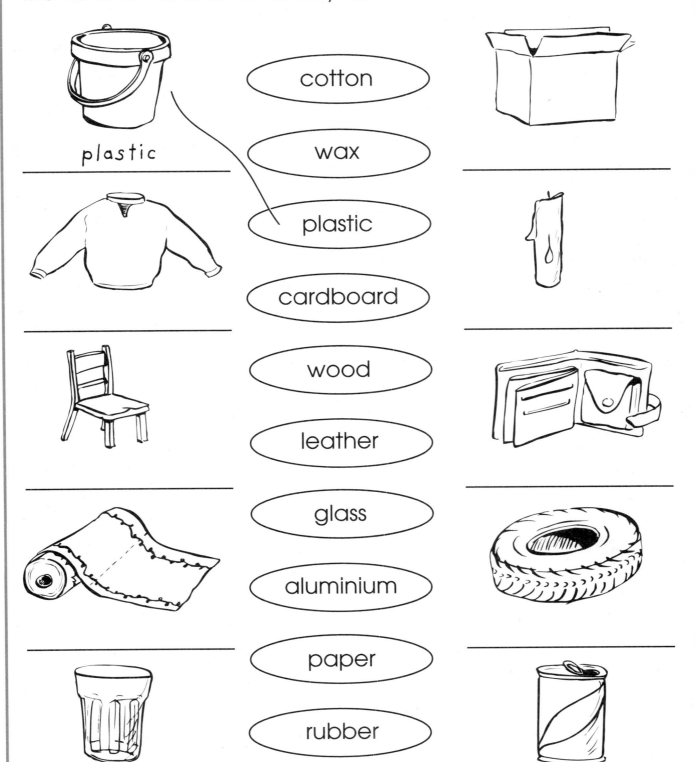

Eating materials

Some **materials** are **edible**. This means that they can be eaten. The edible materials used to make food are called **ingredients**.

Here are the main **ingredients** of some common foods.

Chocolate	**Biscuit**	**Corn flakes**	**Sponge cake**
milk sugar cocoa butter	flour milk sugar salt	sugar salt maize malt	eggs flour milk sugar

Write down which of those foods have the following **ingredients**.

Ingredient	Food name
milk	
flour	
sugar	
salt	

Look at some empty food packets to see what the main ingredients of the food are. Fill in the table below. One has been done for you.

Food name	Main ingredients
tomato soup	tomatoes, cream, sugar, salt

Photocopiable

What is it?

Read the clues carefully. Choose the answer to each clue from the words in the box. The first one has been done for you.

1. A **rubber** bag full of **air**. _balloon_

2. A **metal** pot for boiling water. _____

3. Sheets of **paper** fastened together inside a cover. _____

4. A small rounded **stone**. _____

5. A straight piece of **wood** or **plastic** used for measuring. _____

6. An electric light protected by **glass**. _____

| bulb |
| book |
| ~~balloon~~ |
| kettle |
| pebble |
| ruler |

Now choose the answers to these clues from the words in the box. The answers are all names of **materials**.

1. Water when it is **solid** and **cold**. _____

2. A **transparent liquid**. _____

3. A **hard, rough** material used for building houses. _____

4. Like paper but **stiffer**. _____

5. Forms a white **dust** when crushed. _____

6. Easy to tell by its **taste**. _____

| brick |
| salt |
| ice |
| chalk |
| water |
| card |

SCHOLASTIC
DEVELOPING SCIENCE LANGUAGE for Materials and their properties with 6–7 year olds

What's it like?

The children in Class 2 tested some **materials**.
They wanted to find out about the **features** of each one.
Here are some pictures of the materials they tested.

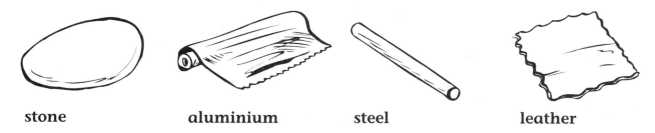

stone   aluminium   steel   leather

First they looked carefully at the four materials. The stone and the leather looked **dull**. The aluminium and the steel looked **shiny**.

Then they felt each material. The stone and the leather felt **rough**. The aluminium and the steel felt **smooth**.

They lifted up each material. The aluminium and the leather felt **light**. The stone and the steel felt **heavy**.

They held a **magnet** close to each material. The stone, the aluminium and the leather did not stick to the magnet. The steel did. The steel was **magnetic**. The other three materials were **not magnetic**.

When the tests were over, the children wrote about what they had done. Their writing showed that different materials have different features or **properties**.

How a material looks and how heavy it is are examples of its properties.

What's it like?

1. Which materials looked **dull**? _____

Which materials looked **shiny**? _____

2. Which materials were **not magnetic**?

_____

3. Circle the correct word to use in each sentence.

The **leather / steel / aluminium** felt **rough**.

The **stone / steel / leather** felt **smooth**.

The **steel / stone / leather** felt **light**.

The **aluminium / steel / leather** felt **heavy**.

4. Fill in this **chart** by writing three **properties** of each material:

Material	Properties
stone	
aluminium	
steel	
leather	

5. Write one more property for each of the four materials.
Use words like **hard**, **soft**, **stiff** and **flexible**.

stone   aluminium   steel   leather

_____   _____   _____   _____

Ask your teacher for an object made from another material.
Test it and write what its properties are.
Have other friends with the same material written the same properties? Why not?

What's it like?

1. How did the stone and the leather look? _____

2. The aluminium looked **shiny**.
   Which other material looked shiny? _____

3. Which material stuck to the magnet? _____

4. Next to each material, write **R** for rough or **S** for smooth.

   steel ◯   leather ◯   stone ◯   aluminium ◯

5. Write in the missing words in these sentences.

   The aluminium felt _____ in weight but the stone felt _____.

   Different materials have different _____.

6. Write either **magnetic** or **not magnetic** below each picture.

   iron   plastic   steel

   _____   _____   _____

7. Can you name three other materials that are **not magnetic**?

   _____   _____   _____

Ask your teacher for an object made from another material, such as plastic. Test its properties.

Photocopiable

Properties crossword

All of these words are properties of materials. Write them in the correct places on the crossword.

smooth	heavy	rough	transparent
firm	stiff	weak	soft
waterproof	light	squashy	hard

Discuss with your friends what all the words mean.

What must it be?

Different **materials** are used for different jobs.
Steel is used for railings because it is strong.
Feathers make pillows feel soft.

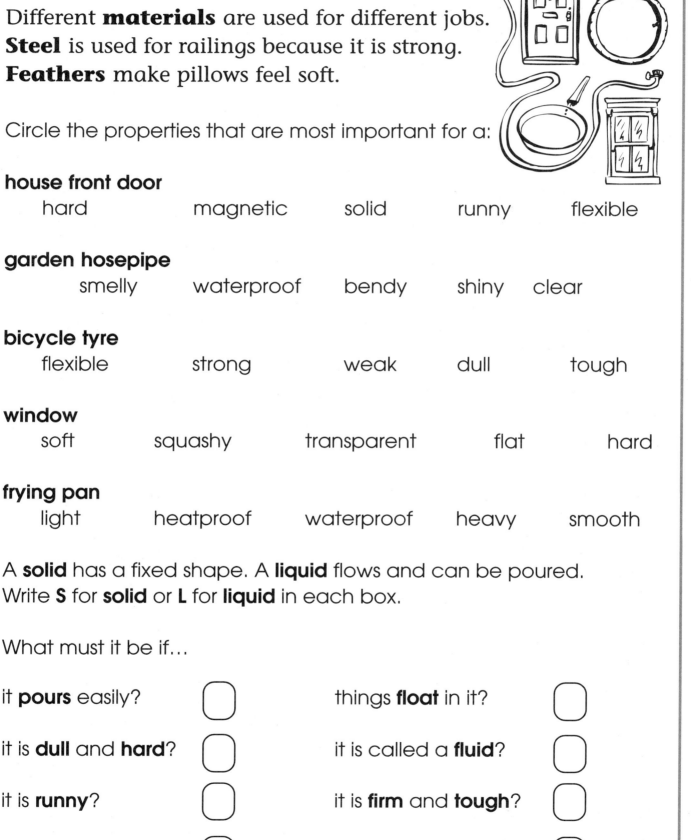

Circle the properties that are most important for a:

house front door

    hard   magnetic   solid   runny   flexible

garden hosepipe

    smelly   waterproof   bendy   shiny   clear

bicycle tyre

    flexible   strong   weak   dull   tough

window

    soft   squashy   transparent   flat   hard

frying pan

    light   heatproof   waterproof   heavy   smooth

A **solid** has a fixed shape. A **liquid** flows and can be poured.
Write **S** for **solid** or **L** for **liquid** in each box.

What must it be if…

it **pours** easily?	☐	things **float** in it?	☐
it is **dull** and **hard**?	☐	it is called a **fluid**?	☐
it is **runny**?	☐	it is **firm** and **tough**?	☐
it is **stiff** and **strong**?	☐	things **sink** in it?	☐

DEVELOPING SCIENCE LANGUAGE for Materials and their properties with 6–7 year olds

Photocopiable

Useful things

Draw a line to connect each picture to its name on the chart. Choose some other objects and write their names in the correct boxes. Do not write any object's name in more than two boxes.

SHINY glossy surface saw blade	DULL no brightness trousers
ROUGH uneven surface brick	SMOOTH even surface TV screen
FLEXIBLE bendy plastic ruler	FIRM does not bend pencil
TRANSPARENT can see through it glass	NOT TRANSPARENT cannot see through it mug
WATERPROOF does not let water through umbrella	NOT WATERPROOF lets water through towel

Enlarge to A3 size if required.

DEVELOPING SCIENCE LANGUAGE for Materials and their properties with 6–7 year olds

Putting things right

Marti and Joss are copying names of objects from a list onto a **diagram**. Can you copy the other names from the list into the correct boxes? Some names may go into more than one box.

| stone |
| postcard |
| ~~carpet~~ |
| wet clay |
| ~~warm Plasticine~~ |
| tree bark |
| wool |
| silk |
| ~~house brick~~ |
| paper towel |
| glass |
| ~~plastic spoon~~ |

	rough	smooth
hard	house brick	plastic spoon
soft	carpet	warm Plasticine

SCHOLASTIC
DEVELOPING SCIENCE LANGUAGE for Materials and their properties with 6–7 year olds

Tell me about it

Write about each **material** and its **properties**.
Use the words at the bottom of the page to help you.

Wood

_____
_____

Plastic

_____
_____

Chocolate

_____
_____

Fabric

_____
_____

Water

_____
_____

Glass

_____
_____

edible   hard   rough   natural   soft

solid   liquid

shiny   weak   smooth   strong   manufactured

What shall we use?

1.

Everything is made from something.
Different things are made from different **materials**.

3.

Some materials are better for some jobs than others. Choosing the right material for the job is important.

5.

Plastic is used for rain gutters and downpipes. It is **tough** and will not **rust**.

2.

Not all materials **look**, **feel**, **smell** or **taste** the same.

4.

Glass is used for windows. It is **smooth** and **transparent**. Materials that are **waterproof** are used to make clothes for wet weather.

6.

Wood is used for furniture. It is **strong** and can easily be cut into **shape**.

What shall we use?

Answer these questions. Use sentences where you can.

1. Are all things made from the same **materials**? _____

2. Do all materials **look, feel, smell** and **taste** the same? _____

3. Why is **glass** used for windows? _____
   _____

4. Which material is **tough**, will not **rust** and is used for rain gutters and downpipes? _____

5. Why is **wood** a good material for making furniture?
   _____
   _____

6. **Glass** is used for windows. What else can glass be used to make?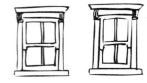
   _____

7. **Waterproof** materials are used to make clothes for wet weather. Name three materials that are waterproof.
   _____

8. **Wood** is used for furniture. Write the names of three other things that can be made from wood.
   _____
   _____

Draw a picture of your house. **Label** the parts with the names of the materials they are made from.

What shall we use?

1. True or false? Everything is made from something. _____

2. Do all materials **look, feel, smell** and **taste** the same? _____

3. Fill in the missing words to complete these sentences.

   • Choosing the right material for the _____ is important.

   • _____ is used for windows. It is _____ and _____ .

4. Why is plastic used for gutters and downpipes?
   _____

5. Name two properties of wood. _____

6. Fill in this chart by writing 'yes' or 'no' in each box.

	glass	car sponge	plastic	aluminium
hard	yes			
soft				no
rough				
smooth		no		
transparent				
waterproof			yes	

 Draw a picture of your house. **Label** the parts to show what they are made from. You might find some of these words useful:

> glass   plastic   wood   brick   slate   stone   concrete

Materials wordsearch

Write the missing letters in the names of these **materials**. The clues will help you to work out each word.

1. A tree is made of this.
2. A doll is made of this.
3. A pin is made of this.
4. You are writing on this.
5. A wall can be built with this.
6. Builders are always making this.
7. Children use this to build castles.
8. This is used for making models.
9. This is used to make clothes.
10. You can see through this.

1. w _ _ d
2. p l _ s t _ c
3. m e _ a _
4. p _ p _ r
5. s t _ n _
6. c _ n c r _ t e
7. s _ _ d
8. c l _ _
9. c o t _ o _
10. g _ a s _

Find the same words in this **wordsearch**. Use a ruler to draw a line in a different colour through each word.

e	k	o	i	d	o	o	w
t	a	q	n	r	i	b	p
e	m	d	m	e	t	a	l
r	j	n	p	p	f	g	a
c	l	a	y	a	c	l	s
n	d	s	h	p	g	a	t
o	e	e	n	o	t	s	i
c	o	t	t	o	n	s	c

Changing shape

The shape of some things can be changed by **bending**, **twisting**, **stretching** or **squashing** them.

Mundeep and Sally tested some materials. They had to find out which materials would **bend**, **twist**, **stretch** or **squash**.

They put their results into a table:

✓ will ✗ will not	bend	squash	stretch	twist
rubber band	✓	✗	✓	✓
wooden pencil	✗	✗	✗	✗
foam sponge	✓	✓	✓	✓
metal wire	✓	✗	✗	✓
plastic ruler	✓	✗	✗	✗
Plasticine	✓	✓	✓	✓

Below the table, they made four drawings to show how a foam sponge can be **bent**, **twisted**, **stretched** and **squashed**.

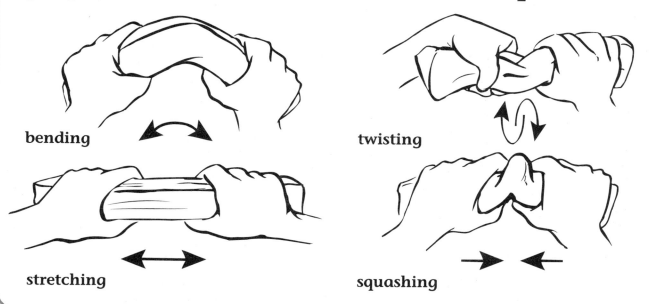

bending

twisting

stretching

squashing

Photocopiable

Changing shape

1. Write four ways in which the **shape** of things can be changed.

   _____
   _____

2. Name a **material** that will:

   bend _____   stretch _____

   twist _____   squash _____

3. Which material tested by Sally and Mundeep will:

   • only bend? _____

   • only bend and twist? _____

   • only bend, twist and stretch? _____

4. Which materials tested by Sally and Mundeep will not:

   • squash? _____

   • twist or stretch? _____

5. What is happening to the materials in these pictures? Write **bending, twisting, stretching** or **squashing** next to each picture.

   _____   _____

   _____   _____

Bend, twist, stretch and **squash** some play dough or Plasticine to make different shapes. Write a card label for each shape to say how you made it.

Changing shape

1. Give **two** ways in which the shape of things can be changed.

   _____ _____

2. Name **two** materials that will:

   bend   stretch

   _____   _____

   _____   _____

   twist   squash

   _____   _____

   _____   _____

   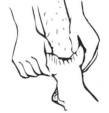

3. Which materials tested by Sally and Mundeep can be changed in all four ways: **bending**, **twisting**, **stretching** and **squashing**?

   _____

4. Which material tested by them will not bend? _____

5. Fill in this table in the same way as Mundeep and Sally.

✓ will ✗ will not	bend	twist	stretch	squash
metal spring				
rock				
paper				

Bend, twist, stretch and **squash** some play dough or Plasticine to make different shapes. Talk with your friends about the shapes you have made.

Bending, twisting, stretching and squashing

Connect each **material** to how its shape can be changed. Some materials can change shape in more than one way.

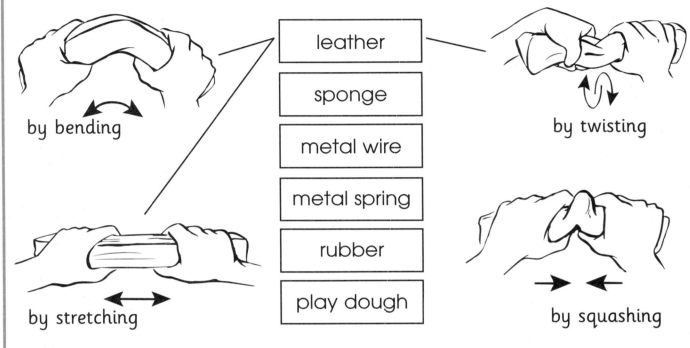

Tick the things that will **bend**.

Circle the things that will **twist**.

Draw a box round the things that will **stretch**.

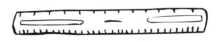  

Cross out the things that will **squash**.

Hot and cold

Things can change when they get very **hot** or very **cold**.

When water gets very hot it **boils**. The water changes into **steam**. When the steam gets **cooler** it changes back into water again.

When water gets very cold it **freezes** and becomes **hard**. The water has changed into **ice**. When the ice gets **warmer** it **melts** back into water again.

Most solids **melt** when they are **heated**. When a **solid** melts it changes into a **liquid**. Butter, chocolate and ice-cream all melt when they are heated.

Some materials get **harder** when they are **heated**. Clay and dough harden when they are baked in a hot oven. When they cool down, they do not become soft again.

Hot and cold

 Answer the first three questions in complete sentences.

1. Which **material** changes into **steam** when it **boils**?
   _____

2. What does a **solid** change into when it **melts**?
   _____

3. What happens to clay or dough when it is baked in a hot oven?
   _____

4. **Ice** and **steam** are both forms of _____.

5. Circle the things that **melt** easily.

| banana | chocolate | bread | ice-cream | butter |

 6. What will happen to **ice** that is left standing in a **warm** classroom?
   _____

7. Circle the pictures that show forms of water.

 Think about the kinds of **food** you eat.
Write a list of them.
Tick the ones that have to be **cooked** (heated) before you can eat them.

Hot and cold

1. Choose the correct word from the box to complete each sentence.

   When water gets very **hot** it _____.

   When water gets very **cold** it _____.

   | freezes |
   | melts |
   | boils |

2. Underline the right word to use in this sentence:

   When **steam** gets **warmer / cooler** it changes into water.

3. True or false? Most **solids melt** when they are **heated**. _____

4. Tick the things that **melt** easily.

    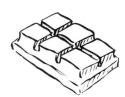   

5. Do clay and dough get **harder** or **softer** when they are baked in a hot oven? _____

6. What happens to **melted** chocolate when it is **cooled**?

   _____

7. Write these words in the correct boxes: **water   ice   steam**

   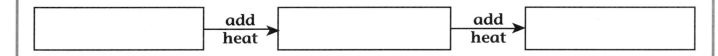

Think about the kinds of **food** you eat. Write a list of the things you have eaten today.

Photocopiable

1 Melt down

You will need: a copy of the 'Melt down graph' sheet (page 53), crayons, a ruler.

Study the graph sheet carefully. Use it to answer these questions.

1. Where was the ice cube that **melted** the fastest?
   _____

2. How long did the ice cube by the door take to **melt**?
   _____

3. Where was the ice cube that **melted** the slowest?
   _____

4. Where was the ice cube that took half an hour to **melt**?
   _____

5. Do you think it was sunny by the window? _____
   Why do you think that?
   _____
   _____

6. Why do you think the three ice cubes took different times to **melt**?
   _____

7. Gill and Tara also put an ice cube into a glass of **warm** tap water. Mark on the graph how long you think this cube took to **melt**.

8. Now try melting an ice cube of your own in **warm** tap water. How long does it take to melt? Was your **prediction** close?

DEVELOPING SCIENCE LANGUAGE for Materials and their properties with 6–7 year olds

Melt down graph

Gill and Tara used three ice cubes to find the **warmest** place in their classroom.

All the ice cubes were the same size.
They put each ice cube on a plate.
They put the three plates in different places in the room.
They measured how long it took for each ice cube to **melt** completely.

Here are their results:

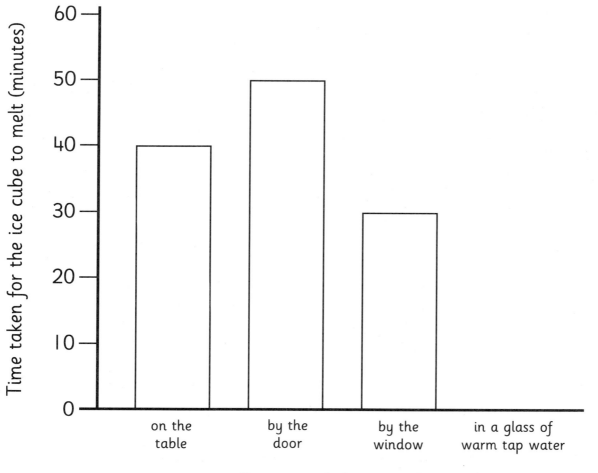

All change

How does **heat** make things **change**?
Some children at North Road School
tried to find out.
Tasneem and John made a clay model.
They **heated** it in an oven. This is called
'firing' the clay.

What do you think the clay looked and felt like:
- before they put it into the oven?

_____

- after being in the oven?

_____

Sam and Pat stirred a cake mixture.
Then they cooked it in an oven.
Describe what you think the
mixture looked like:

- before they cooked it

_____

- after they cooked it

_____

Clay and cake mixture **change** when you **heat** them.
They cannot be **changed back** to how they were before.

What other things do you
know that change when you   _____
heat them and cannot be
changed back?   _____

COVER THESE INSTRUCTIONS WHEN PHOTOCOPYING.

Teacher instructions
Ideally, before working on this sheet, the children should have some experience of:
- modelling with clay and firing their models in an oven
- mixing cake ingredients and baking cakes.

Test it

Sarah and Lee tested some **materials** to see whether they were **waterproof**. Here are the instructions they followed.

To test whether a material is waterproof

You will need:

What to do:
1. Place each material in turn on a surface that is **dry**, **hard** and **shiny**.
2. **Pour** one teaspoonful of water onto the material.
3. Leave it for one minute.
4. Lift up the material very carefully and check whether the surface below it is **dry** or **wet**.
5. Put a ✓ on the chart if the surface is **dry**. Put a ✗ on the chart if the surface is **wet**.

material	waterproof?
paper towel	✗
kitchen foil	✓
empty crisp bag	✓
thin card	✗
cotton T-shirt	✗
plastic bag	✓

Test it

1. What did Sarah and Lee want to find out about each **material**?
   _____

2. What two items of **equipment** were needed for the test?
   _____

3. What kind of **surface** was each material placed on?
   _____

4. How many **teaspoonfuls** of water were used for each test? _____

5. Name the things that Lee and Sarah found to be **waterproof**.
   _____

6. How long was each material left before looking underneath it? _____

7. Why did the **hard, shiny** surface below some of the materials become **wet**?
   _____
   _____

8. How could you make a material **waterproof** that was **not waterproof**?
   _____
   _____
   _____

Test some other **materials** to find out which are **waterproof**. Do the test in the same way as Sarah and Lee. Record your results on a chart or table.

Test it

1. Write the names of three **materials** that Sarah and Lee tested.
   _____

2. Give the names of the two items of **equipment** used in the test.
   _____

3. Shade in the box that has the right words to describe the kind of **surface** each material was placed on.

   | rough, hard | | dull, flexible | | hard, shiny |

4. How many **teaspoonfuls** of water were used for each test? ____

5. Tick the things that Lee and Sarah found to be **waterproof**.

   empty crisp bag ☐   thin card ☐   plastic bag ☐
   cotton T-shirt ☐   kitchen foil ☐ paper towel ☐

6. What did a **wet** surface below a material mean?
   _____

   What did a **dry** surface mean?
   _____

7. What does **waterproof** mean?
   _____

Test some other **materials** to find out which are **waterproof**.
Do the test in the same way as Sarah and Lee.
Ask your teacher to help you draw a chart or table.
Then record your results.

Getting wet

What happens to things when they get **wet**?
Do this **test** to find out.
You are going to put different things in water.
Ask a friend to help you.

You will need: the 'Wetting materials' chart from page 59, a bowl of water, a piece of tissue paper.
You will also need seven other materials, such as: a paper bag, a piece of cardboard, some staples, a squashed can, a piece of fabric, a stick of chalk, a plastic button.

What to do:
On the wetting materials chart:
1. Write your names and your class number.
2. Write the materials to be tested in the **first** column.
3. In the **middle** column, write what you think will happen to each one after an hour in water.

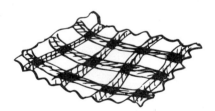 

What to do next:
4. Put all the things in the water. Leave them there for **one hour**.
5. Take the first **material** listed on your chart out of the water.
This should be the tissue paper. Look at it carefully.
Is the chart correct?
6. Take the next material out of the water. Look at it, then fill in the box in the **last** column of your chart.
7. Do the same with the rest of the materials, and fill in the chart.

Our wetting materials chart

Our names _____ Class _____

Fill in this chart with your friend. One row has been done for you.

What we put in water	What we think will happen	What did happen
tissue paper	it will go soggy	it fell to bits

Enlarge this page to A3 size and cut out the chart.

Handling things

You will need one thing made from each of these **materials**: wood, cotton, cardboard, glass, plastic, rubber.

What to do:
Look at and **touch** each **material**. Draw its picture in the correct space below, then write at least two words to describe it. The first picture and words have been done for you.

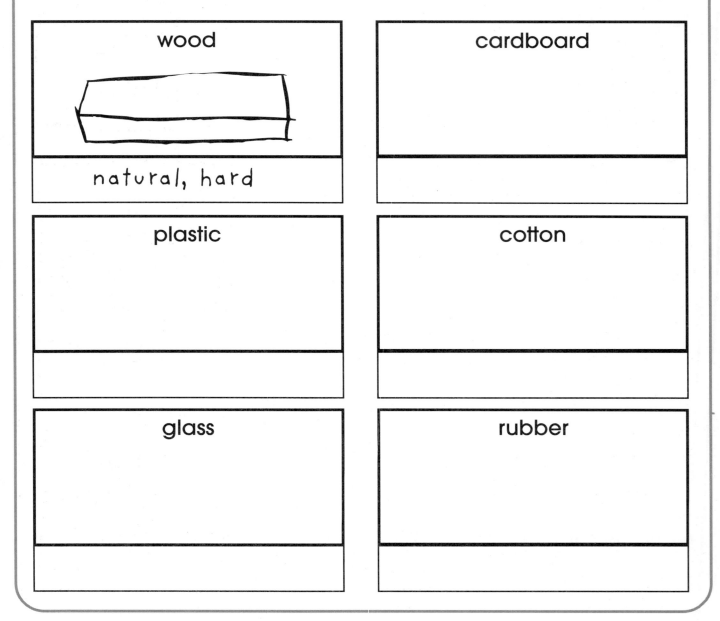

Water

SAVE OUR WATER

Help to **conserve water**.

Make sure you:
- turn off taps
- have a shower and not a bath
- do not use more water than you need when washing your hands
- use a watering can in the garden, not a hose.

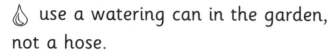

STOP POLLUTION

Do not **pollute** water.

Rivers, ponds, lakes and seas can be kept **clean** by:
- not throwing **litter**
- not pouring **harmful substances** down drains
- not flushing old **medicines** down the toilet
- not using too many garden **fertilisers**

Water

1. How can you save **water** when you are:

 • washing? _____

 • in the garden? _____

2. Write the names of these four different kinds of place that have water and should not be **polluted**.

3. List four things that can **pollute** water.
   _____

4. Find out and write the meaning of each word.
   Use a dictionary to help you.

 • conserve _____

 • pollute _____

 • substance _____

 • fertiliser _____

Make a poster about not wasting water.
Put a title at the top, with words and pictures below.
Ask your teacher if you can display it in your school.

 # Water

1. Here are some ways of saving **water**.
   Can you fill in the missing words?
   - by turning off _____.
   - by having a shower and not a _____.
   - by using a watering _____ in the garden.

2. Match each word to the right picture.

   tap   bath   shower   watering can   plant

3. Circle the names of things that can **pollute** water.

   old medicines   rocks   plants   ducks

   fish   litter   fertiliser   taps

4. Draw a line to connect each word to its meaning.

medicine	to make something dirty
fertiliser	to keep something from harm
pollute	makes plants grow better
conserve	makes you feel better

Make a poster of your own called **Don't Waste Water**.
You may want an adult to help you write your message on it.
Ask your teacher if you can put your poster up in your school.

Using water

Look at each picture. Talk about how **water** is being used. Now write a sentence about how the water is being used in each picture.